MW00681184

INSPIRED

THOUGHTS

SARAH WALZER

8102 Lemont Road,
Suite 300, Woodridge, IL 60517, U.S.A
Phone: 630-268-9900   Fax: 630-268-9500

Copyright © 2002 Great Quotations, Inc.

Compiled by Sarah Walzer

Cover Design by Design Dynamics
Calligraphy by Elizabeth Lucas

Published by Great Quotations, Inc.

Library of Congress Catalog Card Number : 98-075789

ISBN: 1-56245-368-8

Printed in Hong Kong 2002

Too often we get caught up in the daily

activities of life and lose touch with what is

truly important. This collection of quotes

is designed to focus the mind and

stir the soul. Enjoy.

Those who bring sunshine to the lives of others CANNOT KEEP IT FROM THEMSELVES.

James Barrie

The best
and most beautiful
things in the world
cannot be seen,
nor touched . . .
but are felt
in the heart.

HELEN KELLER

Use what talents
you possess.
   The woods would
be very silent if no
birds sang there
except those
   that sang best.

HENRY VAN DYKE

Far away there in the sunshine are my highest aspirations. I may not reach them, but I can look up and see their beauty, believe in them and try to follow where they lead.

LOUISA MAY ALCOTT

Some succeed
because they are
destined to,
but most succeed
because they are
determined to.

It is a funny thing about life ; if you refuse to accept anything but the best, you very often get it.

Somerset Maugham

You can use most any
measure when you're
speaking of success.
You can measure it in
a fancy home, expensive
car or dress.
But the measure of your
real success is one you
cannot spend —
It's the way your
child describes you
when talking to
a friend.

Martin Baxbaum

The great acts of
love are done by
those who are
habitually performing
small acts of kindness.

A friend is
someone who
understands your
past, believes
in your future,
and accepts you
today just the
way you are!

A person's wealth
can be measured
by the love of their
children.

It is one of the most
beautiful compensations
of this life that no man
can sincerely try to help
another without helping
himself.

Ralph Waldo Emerson

Treasure the love
you receive above all.
It will survive long
after your gold and
good health have
vanished.

Og Mandino

Every job is a
self-portrait of
the person who
did it.

The first great gift
we can bestow on others
is a good example.

MORELL

To laugh often and much;
to win the respect of intelligent people
and affection of children; to earn the
appreciation of honest critics and to
endure the betrayal of false friends;
to appreciate beauty, to find the best in
others; to leave the world a bit better,
whether by a healthy child, a garden
patch, or a redeemed social condition;
to know even one life has breathed
easier because you have lived.
This is to have succeeded.

Nothing happens
unless
first a dream.

CARL SANDBURG

Courtesy costs nothing,
yet buys things
that are priceless.

The smallest good deed
is better than the
grandest intention.

You can preach
a better sermon
with your life
than with your lips.

Goldsmith

The journey of a
thousand miles
starts with
a single step.

CHINESE PROVERB

Laughter
is a tranquilizer
with no side effects.

ARNOLD GLASOW

Success
is a journey
not a destination.

Ben Sweetland

Live your life each day
as you would climb a
mountain.

An occasional glance
toward the summit keeps
the goal in mind, but many
beautiful scenes are to be
observed from each new
vantage point.

Climb slowly, steadily,
enjoying each passing
moment; and the view from
the summit will serve as a
fitting climax for the journey.

HAROLD V. MELCHERT

When we have
done our best,
we should
wait the result
in peace.

Love puts
the FUN
in together...
the SAD
in apart...
the HOPE
in tomorrow...
the JOY
in a heart.

26

For every minute
you are angry,
you loose sixty seconds
of
HAPPINESS.

Of all the
things you wear,

your expression
is most
important.

The future
belongs to those
who believe
in the beauty
of their dreams.

Eleanor Roosevelt

The greatest
remedy for anger
is delay.

SENECA

Every charitable act
is a stepping stone
toward heaven.

HENRY WARD BEECHER

There is no beauty

so great

as beauty

shared.

Happiness

is not a state to arrive at,

but a manner

of

traveling.

MARGARET LEE RUNBECK

God grant me

the serenity
to accept the things
I cannot change;
the courage to
change the things
I can, and the
wisdom to know
the difference.

Reinhold Niebuhr

Hope
sees the invisible,
feels the intangible
and achieves the
impossible.

People rarely succeed
at anything
unless they have fun
doing it.

Don't walk
in front of me,
I may not always
follow...

Don't walk
behind me, I may
not always lead...
Just walk beside me
and be my FRIEND.

I can not
change yesterday.
I can only make
the most of today,
and look with hope
toward tomorrow.

There are two ways
of being rich.
One is to have
all you want,
the other is
to be satisfied
with what you have.

Patience is bitter
but its fruit
is sweet.

ᴙ ᴙ ᴙ

People can alter
their lives

✕

by altering
their attitudes.

We make a living
by what we get,
but we make a life
by what we give.

Keep your face
to the sunshine. . .
and you cannot
see the shadows.

HELEN KELLER

One person
with courage
makes a majority.

ANDREW JACKSON

Take Time...

TAKE TIME TO WORK,
IT IS THE PRICE OF SUCCESS.
TAKE TIME TO THINK,
IT IS THE SOURCE OF POWER.
TAKE TIME TO PLAY, IT IS THE
SECRET OF PERPETUAL YOUTH.
TAKE TIME TO BE FRIENDLY,
IT IS THE ROAD TO HAPPINESS.
TAKE TIME TO LOVE
AND BE LOVED, IT IS A
PRIVILEGE OF THE GODS.
TAKE TIME TO SHARE, LIFE IS
TOO SHORT TO BE SELFISH.
TAKE TIME TO LAUGH,
LAUGHTER IS THE MUSIC
OF THE SOUL.

Love
doesn't make the
world go 'round,
but it makes the
ride worthwhile.

Most people
are about as happy
as they make up
their minds to be.

Abraham Lincoln

Finish each day and
be done with it.
You have done what
you could.
Some blunders and
absurdities no doubt creep in.
Forget them as soon
as you can.
Tomorrow is a new day;
You shall begin it
well and serenely;

RALPH WALDO EMERSON

Trust in God.

Believe in yourself.

Dare to dream.

Robert Schuller

Purpose is what gives life a meaning.

It is never
too late to be
what you might
have become.

George Eliot

Your only obligation
in any lifetime
is to be true to yourself.

Richard Bach

A friend
will joyfully sing
with you when you
are on the mountain
top, and silently walk
beside you through
the valley.

All I have seen

teaches me to trust
the creator for
all I have not seen.

RALPH WALDO EMERSON

Happiness

is not the absence of conflict

BUT THE ABILITY

TO COPE WITH IT.

A house is made
   of walls and beams;
a home is built
   with love and dreams.

THE GRAND ESSENTIALS
FOR HAPPINESS ARE:
something to do,
something to love,
and something
to hope for.
— Chalmers

Do more than exist, LIVE.
Do more than touch, FEEL.
Do more than look, OBSERVE.
Do more than read, ABSORB.
Do more than hear, LISTEN.
Do more than listen, UNDERSTAND.
Do more than think, PONDER.
Do more than talk, SAY SOMETHING.

John H. Rhoades

Doubt makes
the mountain
which faith
can move.

Adversity reveals
genius,
prosperity
conceals it.
HORACE

I expect to pass through life
but once.

If, therefore, there be any
kindness I can show, or any good
thing I can do to any fellow being,
let me do it now, as I shall not
pass this way again.

WILLIAM PENN

May you always
find new roads to
travel; new horizons
to explore;
new dreams to call
your own.

The foolish person
seeks happiness
in the distance,
the wise grow it
under their feet.

James Oppenheim

A ship
in a harbor is safe,
but that's not
what ships are
built for.

~·~

64

He who has health,
has hope;
and he who has hope,
has everything.

Arabian Proverb

It takes both
rain and sunshine
to make a rainbow.

Life
is a flower
of which love
is the honey.

LOVE
forgets mistakes.

PROVERBS 17:9

THE WAY
TO HAPPINESS~

Keep your heart

free from from hate,

your mind from worry...

live simply...

expect little...

give much ...

Better keep yourself
clean and bright;
you are the window
through which you
must see the world.

George Bernard Shaw

Inch by inch
life's a cinch.

~~~~~

Yard by yard
life is hard.

A misty morning
does not signify
a cloudy day.

Ancient Proverb

Faith

is the daring of the
soul to go farther
than it can see.

The courage
to speak
must be matched
by the wisdom
to listen.

Well-timed
silence
      hath more
      eloquence
      than speech.
         M. T. Tupper

Oh the comfort,
the inexpressible comfort,
of feeling safe with a person,
having neither to
weigh thoughts nor measure
words, but pouring them all right
out, just as they are,
chaff and grain together;
certain that a faithful hand will
take and sift them, keep what is
worth keeping, and with the
breath of kindness blow the rest
away.

REX COLE

Other Titles by Great Quotations, Inc.

Hard Covers

Ancient Echoes
Behold the Golfer
Commanders in Chief
The Essence of Music
First Ladies
Good Lies for Ladies
Great Quotes From Great Teachers
Great Women
I Thought of You Today
Journey to Success
Just Between Friends
Lasting Impressions
My Husband My Love
Never Ever Give Up
The Passion of Chocolate
Peace Be With You
The Perfect Brew
The Power of Inspiration
Sharing the Season
Teddy Bears
There's No Place Like Home

Paperbacks

301 Ways to Stay Young
ABC's of Parenting
Angel-grams
African American Wisdom
Astrology for Cats
Astrology for Dogs
The Be-Attitudes
Birthday Astrologer
Can We Talk
Chocoholic Reasonettes
Cornerstones of Success
Daddy & Me
Erasing My Sanity
Graduation is Just the Beginning
Grandma I Love You
Happiness is Found Along the Way
Hooked on Golf
Ignorance is Bliss
In Celebration of Women
Inspirations
Interior Design for Idiots

Great Quotations, Inc.
8102 Lemont Road,
Suite 300, Woodridge, IL 60517, U.S.A.
Phone: 630-268-9900   Fax: 630-268-9500

Other Titles by Great Quotations, Inc.

Paperbacks

I'm Not Over the Hill
Life's Lessons
Looking for Mr. Right
Midwest Wisdom
Mommy & Me
Mother, I Love You
The Mother Load
Motivating Quotes
Mrs.Murphy's Laws
Mrs. Webster's Dictionary
Only A Sister
The Other Species
Parenting 101
Pink Power
Romantic Rhapsody
The Secret Langauge of Men
The Secret Langauge of Women
The Secrets in Your Name
A Servant's Heart
Social Disgraces
Stress or Sanity
A Teacher is Better Than
Teenage of Insanity
Touch of Friendship
Wedding Wonders
Words From the Coach

Perpetual Calendars

365 Reasons to Eat Chocolate
Always Remember Who Loves You
Best Friends
Coffee Breaks
The Dog Ate My Car Keys
Extraordinary Women
Foundations of Leadership
Generations
The Heart That Loves
The Honey Jar
I Think My Teacher Sleeps at School
I'm a Little Stressed
Keys to Success
Kid Stuff
Never Never Give Up
Older Than Dirt
Secrets of a Successful Mom
Shopoholic
Sweet Dreams
Teacher Zone
Tee Times
A Touch of Kindness
Apple a Day
Golf Forever
Quotes From Great Women
Teacher Are First Class